THE OLD CATERER'S
FAVORITE HORS D'OEUVRES

THE OLD CATERER'S
FAVORITE HORS D'OEUVRES

by Dot Winters

BRYCE
CULLEN
PUBLISHING

Cover drawing by Don Glitsis.

BRYCE
CULLEN
PUBLISHING

PO Box 731
Alpine, NJ 07620
brycecullen.com

ISBN 978-1-935752-08-0

Library of Congress Control Number: 2011933971

Printed in the United States of America

10 9 8 7 6 5 4 3 2 1

This book is dedicated to my three children, Sherri, Karen, and Doug (Bud),
who have stood behind all my decisions, good or bad,
and to Emily, Sarah, and Brett, my grandchildren,
who have made it all worthwhile.

FOREWORD

For forty odd years I was in training for a catering career without even realizing it. Being raised in a really extended South Carolina family and having charming, gracious parents who loved to entertain was a pretty good start. We gave parties for the family, for the church, for civic groups, and for friends, at both the house in town and our house at the lake. And I helped.

When I married this tall, handsome, Ohio Yankee army officer, I continued the family tradition of giving the best parties around. We lived in several states and by the time our three children were in high school, my husband was a vice president of an international Ohio company, we had a lovely home and I was giving even more elaborate parties. We entertained people from several other countries and my job was to give the good little cocktail parties.

All of this came to an abrupt halt when my husband insisted on a divorce so he could marry one of my "good" friends. I would have to start over with the rest of my life! I was terrified!

It wasn't until my daughter's boyfriend gave me a copy of *How to Get a Man After You're Forty*, as a joke, that I knew what to do. It simply stated that when you found yourself in my position, you get out and do what you love and do best. CATERING! It was like a neon sign flashing over and over.

I moved to Columbus, Ohio, and found this very nice lady who was just starting a catering business. Mary Puchstein never did tell me whether I was hired or not. I just kept working and later, I even bought into the business. I ran away a few times and tried to lead a normal life but kept getting sucked back into the catering game. I loved and hated this monster of a life called Creative Cuisine. It ain't no game for sissies and the minute I reached retirement age, I bolted for the door and never looked back.

I ran in the direction of the beautiful New York Finger Lakes. I now live in an apartment overlooking a lake and attached to, what my friend, Maris, calls the Doctor Seuss House. It is inhabited by my daughter, Karen, her husband, Paul, their two teenage daughters, Emily and Sarah, and about a million animals...but that's another book....

After finally escaping from eighteen years in the catering business, I thought I would never want to cook party food again, but I guess it's like good sex: it's pretty hard to forget. Since hors d'oeuvres were always my biggest food obsession and I seem to have forgotten all about good sex, let's do some of those special party foods. These are tried, some tired, but all are well tested and served many times over the years. I hope you find at least a few you will make over and over.

Let's start with some basic ones ....

DIPS & SAUCES

COLD DIPS

HOT DIPS

SAUCE ONES

The spreaders

Cheese ones

Seafood spreaders

Meat & vegetable spreaders

PICKUPS

IN THE DOUGH

SQUARE PICKUPS

SPREAD-ON BREAD PICKUPS

STAB 'UMS

ROUND STAB 'UMS

STAB 'UMS IN BACON

SKEWERED STAB 'UMS

COLD SKEWERED STAB 'UMS

MISCELLANEOUS FAVORITES

Dips & Sauces

Cold Dips

Dill Dip

This may be the oldest dip known to man, but it still tastes pretty darn good with vegetables, chips, or pretzels.

1 cup sour cream
1 cup mayonnaise
2 tsp. dried parsley flakes
1 Tbs. dried onion flakes
2 Tbs. dried dill weed
2 tsp. Beau Monde seasoning or celery salt to taste

Mix and chill for several hours before serving.
Serve with the above-mentioned things.

Charleston Crab Dip

Years ago, when I had a lovely dinner at The Sea Captain's House in Murrell's Inlet, SC, they served little bowls of this on each table. When I asked what was in it, the waitress brought me a preprinted card with the recipe. It's that good.

1 cup good crab meat, picked over well for shells
1 and 1/4 cups mayonnaise
1/2 cup sharp grated cheddar cheese
4 Tbs. bottled French dressing
1 heaping tsp. horseradish
Juice of half a lemon

Just mix it up and enjoy with good crackers or as a dip for vegetables.

Wendy's Cucumber Dip

This is not old, but it surely was good when Wendy served it at Bunco.

2 large cucumbers
1/2 cup vinegar
2 tsp. salt
2 8-ounce packages of cream cheese
3/4 cup mayonnaise
1 clove garlic, minced

Peel and grate cucumber. Mix with the vinegar and salt, cover and refrigerate overnight. When ready to serve, mix really well with the cream cheese, mayonnaise, and garlic. Squeeze all liquid from the cucumber and mix the pulp with the cheese mixture. Serve with cold vegetables or corn chips.

Spinach Mayonnaise

This was one of the many recipes that Mary had on file when I first went to work for her. I love it and still make it often.

1 10-ounce box frozen chopped spinach, thawed and squeezed dry
1 Tbs. chopped dried parsley
1 Tbs. chopped dried chives
1 tsp. dried tarragon
1 tsp. dry mustard
2 cups mayonnaise

This is good on almost anything. When I say to serve with good crackers, I mean the unflavored ones like Carr's Water Crackers, Breton's, etc. Please don't use chicken-in-whatever fake-tasting ones.

Hummus bi Tahini

This is the old basic recipe, which has now been bastardized with black beans, red beans, blue beans, or whatever you please.

1 can chick peas (drain but save liquid in case needed to thin)
1 clove crushed garlic
1/3 cup tahini (sesame paste)
1/3 cup fresh lemon juice, or to taste
2 Tbs. virgin olive oil
Salt to taste
Chopped fresh parsley to garnish

I use the processor for this. Put in everything except parsley and process until smooth. If you think it needs to be thinner, add chickpea liquid as needed. Put on a pretty platter and sprinkle with parsley, or you can also use crushed red pepper flakes. Serve with pita bread wedges, toasted if you like. Also good served with bread cubes, as in hollow out a loaf of unsliced bread, fill cavity with hummus, and serve with bread cubes.

An apple a day does not necessarily
keep the doctor away,
but a glass or two of wine might.

Great Spinach Dip

I don't know if Mrs. Knorr created this or not, but it's one of my very favorites. The first time I had this at a party in Columbus, Ohio, I sat by the bowl and just ate, ignoring all those tacky people. I don't even remember who they were, but I remember this dip.

1 cup mayonnaise
1 1/2 cups sour cream
1 package Knorr vegetable soup mix
4 green onions, chopped fine
1 can water chestnuts, diced
1 10-ounce package of frozen chopped spinach, thawed and drained

Mix well and chill. Stir again before serving with vegetables, crackers, or in a bread bowl with bread cubes.

Our Clam Dip

This is the only recipe of my ex-mother-in-law's that I ever actually wanted. She is now 97 years old and I pray she has given up cooking.

2 8-ounce packages cream cheese, at room temp. and softened
3 or 4 cans minced clams, drain but save liquid
1 clove garlic, pressed or finely minced
Juice of half a lemon (or more)
Tabasco to taste
Salt and white pepper to taste
Clam liquid until you think it is thin enough to dip

We all stand around and taste this. Whatever is left is served with chips.

Dot's Necessary Dip

I make this dip with this great sauce/marinade that I saw on television years ago. It's really good with meats such as roast pork tenderloin or turkey breasts cut into cubes. First you have to make the sauce, which follows this recipe.

1 cup Hellmann's mayonnaise
1/4 cup Dot's Necessary Sauce
Tabasco sauce to taste

Just mix it up and enjoy.

Dot's Necessary Sauce

This makes a thin sauce, which can be used to marinate meats, to serve at the table, and to baste meats while cooking. It makes a wonderful Bloody Mary.

1 cup water
1/2 cup catsup
1 1/2 cups red wine vinegar
1/2 cup white wine
3 Tbs. yellow mustard
3 Tbs. Worcestershire sauce
3 Tbs. brown sugar, packed
3 Tbs. salt
1 Tbs. black pepper
1 Tbs. red pepper flakes

Put all in a nonreactive pan and bring to a boil. Simmer (uncovered) for half an hour. Store in jars in the fridge.

Nice garnishes are mandatory in the presentation of these recipes.

Hot Dips

Ann Thompson's Bean Dip

Ann was famous for this in Mansfield, Ohio, where she gave lovely cocktail parties. When she retired and moved, she gave me this recipe but made me promise never to share it. That was back in the '60s so, sorry, Ann, if you are still around. It's too good not to share.

8 cups dried pinto beans
6 cloves garlic, chopped or crushed
3 large onions, chopped
Water to cover and add more when needed
1 pound melted butter
2 pounds sharp cheese, grated
Lots of salt

Hot Sauce for Ann Thompson's Bean Dip

1/2 cup or more of fresh jalapeno peppers, finely diced
2 or more cloves garlic, crushed
6 limes, rolled and squeezed for juice (can add lemon juice with lime)
lots of salt to taste

Cover beans, onions, and garlic with water in a large, heavy pot. Cook until tender, adding water as needed, but remember, this is a dip, not soup. Add salt to taste. Cream the beans with a mixer while warm. Add cheese and butter. Add hot sauce but save a little to float on top of dip. Serve in a chafing dish with corn chips.

Cheater's Bean Dip

2 cans pinto beans (drained a little if there is a lot of liquid)
1 onion, chopped
1 clove garlic, pressed or minced
Salt to taste
1/2 stick butter
1/2 pound sharp cheddar, grated
Lime juice to taste
Pickled Jalapeno peppers, crushed

Saute onion and garlic in the butter until soft but not brown. Add beans and cook for 10 minutes or so, stirring often, adding salt to taste. Mash beans and add cheese, butter, lime juice, and peppers. Add the peppers a few at a time until it tastes hot enough. Serve with corn chips.

Chipped Beef Dip

The artful, creative hostess used to put this into a glass pie plate, stand Ritz crackers around the rim, and bake it. Come to think of it, it did look kind of neat.

1 8-ounce package cream cheese
2 Tbs. milk
1 5-ounce jar of chipped beef, diced
2 Tbs. finely chopped green onion
1/4 cup chopped green pepper
1/2 cup of sour cream

Chili con Queso

2 pounds Velveeta cheese
2 cans Rotel Diced Tomatoes and Green Chilis (20 ounces)
1 onion, diced fine
1 cup diced green pepper
1 cup diced red pepper
2 Tbs. butter
Hot sauce or diced jalapeno pepper if you want it hotter

Saute the vegetables in butter. Strain the rotel, but save the liquid to thin, if needed. Cut the cheese up some and mix all in a casserole. Heat in microwave, stirring a few times, until melted and hot. Taste and adjust seasonings. Serve with corn chips. Good with blanched broccoli too.

Hot Chili Dip

The canned tamales make this very different.

2 pounds lean ground beef
2 large onions, chopped
2 tsp. salt
4 Tbs. chili powder
1 Tbs. cumin
1 tsp. red pepper flakes
1 (1 pound 12 ounce) can of tomato puree
1 cup water, if needed
2 cans tamales, unwrapped and mashed up some
Grated cheddar cheese for topping
Chopped green onion for topping

Brown beef and onions in a heavy pot. Add all ingredients up to the water. Add water and cook for an hour or so like you would your favorite chili. Taste for seasonings and adjust if needed. Add mashed tamales and stir well to thicken the dip. Serve in a chafer with cheese and onions on top. Serve with corn chips.

My grandson, Brett, loves this. He's a six-year-old chili head.

Hot Artichoke Dip

This is my method of making this to keep a nice chunky texture and a consistent taste. Add whatever strikes you at the moment.

1 can artichokes, drained, chopped, and measured
Mayonnaise to equal measured artichokes
Parmesan cheese to equal measured artichokes
Several dashes of Tabasco

Mix it up, bake at 375 degrees in a nice little sprayed casserole for about 20 minutes, or until hot and bubbly. Serve with your favorite crackers. Double or triple the recipe if you are having a party.

When you see a guest make a face
when she tastes your latest creation,
consider that she might not have
an educated palate like you do.

Dot's Seafood Newburg

I created this one time when a lady wanted a hot cheese crab dip that wasn't yellow in color. We sold gallons and gallons of this good stuff.

1 cup butter
1 cup flour
3 cups rich chicken broth
3 cups half and half
1-1/2 pounds sharp white cheddar (Black Diamond is a good one), grated
Salt and white pepper to taste
Dry sherry to taste
2 pounds or more of your choice of cooked seafood, cut up some
2 large cans of sliced mushrooms
(about the only time I suggest canned mushrooms)
You may use fresh sauteed ones, of course.

I like to use a large double boiler for this so you can't burn it. Melt butter and add flour. Cook for several minutes to be sure flour is cooked. Add liquids slowly, using a whisk. Add salt, pepper, and the grated cheese.

Let this cook for five minutes or so and add the well drained mushrooms, seafood, and sherry. Taste and adjust seasonings. You may want to add a little hot sauce or lemon juice, but I like it straight up. Serve with toast points or little toast cups. This fills about fifty little cups. (Trim crust from cheap white bread, roll with rolling pin, push into mini muffin tins, and bake.)

SAUCE ONES

Dill Sauce for Salmon

2 cups mayonnaise
2 Tbs. dry dill weed
Seasoned salt to taste (try 1 tsp. first)
1 Tbs. fresh lemon juice
2 Tbs. oil to thin a little
Mix ahead of serving so flavors
can blend. Good served with
smoked salmon along with chopped red onion, capers
and party rye.

Mom's White Sauce for Shrimp

I don't know who's Mom this was, but she was certainly creative when she ran out of Ketchup.

1 cup mayonnaise
2 Tbs. lemon juice
Salt to taste...1/2 tsp. or so
1/4 tsp, paprika
1/4 cup chopped fresh parsley
1/2 tsp. Worcestershire sauce
1 Tbs. grated onion
1 Tbs. snipped chives
1 clove garlic, minced
1 Tbs. capers
1/2 cup sour cream

Mix well, taste, and adjust seasonings.

Remoulade Sauce for Seafood

2 cups mayonnaise

1 hardboiled egg, diced

2 Tbs. chopped green onion

1 Tbs. capers

1 tsp. anchovy paste

1 tsp. dried tarragon

2 tsp. Dijon mustard

Mix and serve with seafood. Remember to not keep for many days with the egg in it. Can omit egg.

Sauce Louis for Seafood

1 cup mayonnaise
1 tsp. horseradish
1/3 cup bottled red French dressing
1 tsp. Worcestershire sauce
1/4 cup chili sauce
salt and white pepper to taste
2 Tbs. minced green onion
2 Tbs. minced green olives

This is good with seafoods other than the famous Crab Louis.

My Cocktail Sauce

1/2 cup ketchup
Pinch of salt
1 generous Tbs. prepared horseradish
Tabasco sauce to taste
1 Tbs. fresh lemon juice
1/2 tsp. Worcestershire sauce

Can use chili sauce with this same recipe, but ketchup is always around. You will want to make several recipes of this, of course.

Pine Nut Sauce for Shrimp

This is different and really good.

1/3 cup toasted pine nuts
3 hard boiled eggs, cut up
1 cup sour cream
1/4 cup mayonnaise
2 Tbs. fresh lime juice
2 Tbs. ground coriander
Salt to taste

Mix in processor and chill. Serve with cocktail shrimp.

The Spreaders

These are my most favorite ones. I like to see how much I can pile on a cracker. Let's start with...

CHEESE ONES

Sister Peg's Jeweled Cheese Ball

Peg made this for a beach trip and Cecil made her Peking Pecans (as in Cecil's Peking Pecans) and I became pretty piggish.

2 cups (8 oz.) shredded cheddar cheese
1 cup pitted dates, chopped (don't use the ones rolled in sugar)
1 stick butter, softened
1 Tbs. brandy
1/2 cup toasted sliced almonds

In a 1-1/2 quart mixing bowl, combine all ingredients except nuts. Beat at medium speed, scraping bowl often, until well mixed. Shape into a ball and roll in nuts. Cover and chill until one-half hour before serving with crackers.

Boursin Cheese

There have been about a million of these recipes around, but this is the one we used for catering.

2 8-ounce packages cream cheese
2 sticks butter, softened
1/2 tsp. each of oregano, thyme, marjoram, dill, basil, and garlic powder
1 tsp. cracked black pepper

Mix well and chill. We made it in a mold, then frosted and decorated with softened cream cheese. Serve with crackers. Can also form into a flat ball and roll in more cracked pepper.

Cheese thoughts.

When you make a plate of cheese for a party, try to remember to make it user friendly (a favorite catering term... sounds so wise). What it means is to not make this a chore for the guests, as in cut those cheeses up in cubes, little wedges, little sticks so people don't have to spend a lot of time cutting the cheese. I try to only leave the nice, soft, and spreadable ones in big pieces.

Nutted Cheese Ring

This serves about 25 people, so plan to make it for a party.

2 pounds finely grated sharp cheddar cheese
1 small onion, grated
1 cup mayonnaise
1/2 to 1 tsp. cayenne pepper
1 cup chopped pecans, toasted
Strawberry preserves for center of ring

Put the cheese, onion, red pepper, and mayo into a large bowl and mix well. Spray a one-quart ring mold with Pam and lay a few strips of plastic wrap in mold, leaving flaps on inside and outside of ring to help in removing cheese from ring. Put the pecans into the bottom of mold. Then put the cheese mixture into a processor in several batches, putting into the mold after each batch. Push down to distribute well. Try not to disturb the nuts too much. Cover ring with plastic wrap and chill well. Unmold onto a pretty plate, decorate with greens (I like curly endive) and fresh strawberries if you like. Place a small bowl in center of ring for the strawberry preserves and put a little spoon in preserves. Serve with spreaders for cheese and crackers to spread it on.

East Indian Cheese Ball

This is from the Dispatch newspaper in Columbus, Ohio, many years ago.

16 ounces of softened cream cheese
1 cup chopped peanuts
1 cup well drained small-curd cottage cheese
1 cup raisins
1 tsp. curry powder
1/2 cup shredded coconut
1 cup finely chopped green onions
3/4 cup of Major Grey's chutney

Beat cream cheese, cottage cheese, and curry powder with electric mixer until smooth. Beat in the remaining ingredients, except chutney, by hand. Form into a ball and wrap in waxed paper. Chill at least six hours. To serve, place on a platter, and make an indentation in top to hold chutney. Place some greens around and spoon chutney on top. Serve with toasted pita triangles or crackers.

Baked Party Brie

Whole brie of any size
Brown sugar
Sliced almonds

Spray a pretty, round, flat casserole and place the unpeeled brie in it. Sprinkle generously with brown sugar and then with the almonds. Bake at 375 degrees or 15 to 20 minutes or until hot and bubbly. Serve with unflavored crackers.

Puff Pastry Baked Brie

Whole brie of any size
Frozen puff pastry, enough to encase the brie
Strawberry (or any) preserves
Melted butter or egg wash to brush top and sides

Place a piece of the thawed puff pastry on a floured surface and roll out some. Place the brie on the pastry and spoon on enough preserves to mound a little on the brie. Either pull up the sides of the pastry to cover the brie like a pouch or place another piece of pastry on top and crimp the edges to encase the brie. Decorate the top with extra pastry and brush with butter or egg wash. Bake at 375 degrees until puffed and browned some, 15 to 20 minutes, according to brie size and your oven. In other words, watch it. Serve with crackers or you can just let people cut pieces, but it's messy.

SEAFOOD SPREADERS

Gourmet Crab Mold

1 tsp. unflavored gelatin
3/4 tsp. seasoned salt
1/4 cup cold water
1 2-ounce jar pimientos, diced
16-ounce package softened cream cheese
6 ounces well-drained crab meat
2 Tbs. dry sherry
1/8 tsp. black pepper
1/4 cup chopped fresh parsley

Soften gelatin in water and put <u>over</u> boiling water to dissolve. Beat cream cheese, sherry, and gelatin, mixing well. Fold everything else gently to combine. Put into a three-cup greased mold to chill. Unmold and decorate on a pretty plate. Serve with good crackers.

Shrimp Butter

We must have sold a billion pounds of this one. This serves about 25 with other party foods. My Sarah craves this one and my niece, Beth, just called me from Colorado to get this recipe for a party she was having.

1 pound (or more) cooked and cleaned shrimp, processed until chunky
1 pound cream cheese, softened
2 sticks butter, softened
4 Tbs. mayonnaise
2 Tbs. grated onion
1 small clove pressed garlic
Salt, white pepper, fresh lemon juice and Tabasco to taste.

Cream butter and cream cheese together and mix in other ingredients to blend really well with electric mixer. You can put this into a fish-type mold or serve it in a bowl with some of those good, unflavored crackers.

Salmon Tartar

Serves 25 with other party foods. This is wonderful if you like smoked salmon. Just plain good if you don't.

1 small onion, chopped
2 Tbs. lime juice
2 green onions, chopped
2 Tbs. good olive oil
1 clove garlic, minced
Salt to taste
2/3 cup fresh chopped parsley
1-1/2 pounds smoked salmon, processed in batches
2 tsp. dried tarragon
Grated rind of one lime
1 tsp. white pepper

Make sure the salmon is really cold. Cut fish up some before processing in batches. Put into a bowl and fold all ingredients and mix together. Serve with party rye. Great on cucumber slices.

Never let your guests see you
sweat or pick your teeth.

Shrimp Mold

This is also good served as a buffet luncheon dish. Use whole small shrimp for buffet dish.

1 pound cooked and cleaned shrimp
Juice of 1 lemon
2 cans tomato soup
1/2 cup fresh chopped parsley
2 packets plain gelatin and 1/2 cup water
2 Tbs. each finely chopped onion, celery, and red pepper
8-ounce package cream cheese, softened
1 cup mayonnaise
Hot sauce to taste

Chop shrimp up some. Dissolve gelatin in water. Heat soup and add gelatin to dissolve. Take off heat and beat in cream cheese until well mixed with soup. Add all other ingredients and put into a pretty greased mold. Chill well and serve garnished nicely.

Salmon Mousse

This is also good for a first course if you are having a formal dinner. Just put it in nice little molds.

1 envelope Knox gelatin
1/2 cup liquid from canned salmon
1 cup canned red salmon (picked over)
1 cup mayonnaise
2 Tbs. fresh lemon juice
1/2 tsp. paprika
1 medium onion, chopped
2 tsp. dry dill weed
1/2 cup sour cream
Water if needed to extend salmon juice to
1/2 cup of liquid.

Soften gelatin in lemon juice. Dissolve in boiling salmon liquid. Mix all ingredients in a bowl. In batches, put in processor, and then transfer to well-oiled fish-shaped mold. Chill overnight. Unmold, put on greens and decorate nicely. Is good with party rye or rye crackers.

MEAT & VEGETABLE SPREADERS

Mushroom Pâté

This is from Bette Rosbotton, who had a cooking school at Lazarus's downtown department store in Columbus, Ohio. She has a food column in the Columbus Dispatch and at least one published cookbook. I enjoyed this at a cooking class at Lazarus.

4 Tbs. unsalted butter
8 ounces mushrooms, cleaned and finely chopped
(save 1 or 2 out)

2 tsp. finely chopped garlic
1/4 cup mild onion, finely chopped
1/3 cup of strong chicken broth
4 ounces cream cheese, room temperature
Salt and pepper to taste
Parsley, chopped green onion tops or chives to garnish
Toast points

Melt half of butter in skillet and saute mushrooms for two or three minutes. Add onion and garlic and saute one more minute. Add the chicken broth and cook over high heat until all liquid has evaporated, four or five minutes. Let cool to room temperature before adding to cream cheese and other half of butter, which has been beaten together. Add salt and pepper, taste and adjust seasonings. Put in a pretty little bowl, cover with plastic wrap and chill. Add garnish of your choice and serve with toast points. It is also good to save a few sliced mushrooms for garnish so your guests won't have to ask.

Bud's Caponata

I combined several recipes to create this. My son, Bud, loves this. He's due for a big batch. I'll have to send Debbie, his wife, this recipe or maybe give them a copy of this book. This makes a lot, but it keeps for weeks in the fridge and you can use it as a vegetable, salad, first course, a snack, or almost anything before dessert.

2 medium eggplant, peeled and cut into 1-inch cubes
Salt and pepper to taste
2 medium onions, chopped
3 or 4 Tbs. capers
2 cloves garlic, minced
1 6-ounce jar green olives, sliced
1/4 cup olive oil
2 14-ounce cans diced tomatoes
2 green peppers, coarsely chopped
1 8-ounce can tomato sauce
1 or 2 small zucchini, coarsely chopped
1/4 cup red wine vinegar
2 cups coarsely chopped celery
1 Tbs. sugar
2 tsp. dried basil

Put oil into heavy pot and saute eggplant, onion, and garlic until soft but not browned. Add the other ingredients and simmer covered for about half an hour. Uncover and cook until thick, but don't let it burn after all that work. Taste and adjust seasonings. Chill and serve with toasted pita bread wedges.

Steak Tartar

I made this once and asked Tay, my nephew, to taste and tell me what it needed. He tasted and said, "That needs cooking!"

2 pounds trimmed beef tenderloin
1-1/2 tsp. salt
1 large sweet onion, minced
1 tsp. black pepper, freshly ground
1/2 cup drained capers
1/4 cup fresh chopped parsley
1/3 cup brandy
2 tsp. Dijon mustard
2 Tbs. olive oil
Dash of Worcestershire and Tabasco

I like to grind my own beef for tartar, so I cube up the tenderloin in one-inch cubes and stick in the freezer until it's really cold. Then I process it in small batches, removing to a bowl to mix everything in. Can put into sprayed mold and chill, or serve mounded on a plate of greens garnished with anchovies and little pickles. Good served on crackers or party rye.

When attending a party,
always ask the hostess for
at least one of her recipes.
It makes her feel special and you
really don't have to ever make it.

Chicken Liver Pâté

1 pound chicken livers, rinsed and trimmed
1 cup onions, chopped
1/2 stick butter
3 hard boiled eggs, cut up some
2 Tbs. mayonnaise
2 Tbs. brandy
Salt and pepper to taste

Saute livers and onions in the butter until the livers are no longer pink in the middle. Process the livers in a couple of batches, using off-on method, adding eggs. Put in a bowl and add the rest, mixing well. Put into a sprayed mold and chill. Serve on a bed of greens with cornichons or dill pickles. Serve with party rye or your favorite plain crackers.

PICKUPS

The Antipasto Tray

You should always consider this as your main item at a big party or for just a few friends. I have found that you only have to polish or dust off a few trays and you only have to wash and put away a few. I like to line the whole tray with greens, like curly endive that won't wilt before the guests arrive. Consider the cheeses (cut into cubes and nice little pick-me-up shapes), olives, Italian type meats, marinated items and anything else you like. Get out all those opened jars of pickled pig's feet and tripe. If they are messy, put them into tiny bowls that will fit on your tray. Cluster toothpicks among the greens and provide crackers and breads. Your food is almost done and it looks like you have been on a world-wide shopping tour for your party.

Roquefort Grapes

1 pound seedless grapes of your choice
1 8-ounce package cream cheese, softened
4 ounces crumbled Roquefort (or blue) cheese
A little cream or milk
1-1/2 cups toasted, chopped nuts of your choice

Mix cream cheese and blue cheese well, adding a little cream to thin. Pick grapes from stems, wash and dry really well. Roll each grape in cheese and then in the nuts. Have a pretty tray with some greens on it ready to place grapes back into a cluster shape. Grape leaves are great to garnish with if possible. A cluster of these would be really nice on that antipasto tray. These are eaten with the fingers, of course.

Cecil's Peking Pecans

My favorite (and only) sister-in-law made these to take to the Isle of Palms in SC and I couldn't stop eating them. It wasn't long until I was on the phone from New York, begging for the recipe.

3/4 stick butter
1 pound pecan halves
2 Tbs. Kikkoman's soy sauce
2 tsp. salt
1/4 to 1/2 tsp. black pepper

Preheat oven to 300 degrees. Melt butter in a rimmed cookie sheet and add nuts. Bake for 30 minutes. Check if your oven is high. Cool a little, add remaining seasonings, and toss.

In the Dough

100 Mini Quiches

You will need at least two mini-muffin pans if you decide to try these. First make the dough and chill it.

Dough for 50
2 cups butter, softened
12 ounces cream cheese, softened
4 cups flour

This is easy to make if you use a processor, but you may have to make it in a couple of batches. Just mix it up to form a ball, wrap and chill.

Form into 1-1/2-inch balls and press them into greased muffin pans. Fill shells with any of below-mentioned goodies and pour in the quiche liquid to fill the crust almost to the rim. The secret to pouring the liquid just into shells, I have found, is to put liquid, in batches, into a soft plastic picnic drinking cup. Don't pour, just squeeze sides to milk it in. You don't lose many drops this way.

Classic Quiche Liquid for 50
3 cups half and half
6 eggs
1-1/2 tsp. salt
Fresh grated nutmeg (10 or 12 gratings or 1/4 tsp. powdered nutmeg)
Dash of cayenne pepper
Dash of white or black pepper

Beat eggs really well with other ingredients.
The blender works really well.

Fillings

Quiche Lorraine
Finely chopped, cooked bacon and finely grated Swiss Cheese, about a pound of each for 50 minis.

Apple and Bleu Cheese
Peeled and chopped Granny Smith Apple and crumbled bleu cheese.

Crab and Swiss
Picked over crab and finely grated Swiss.

Spinach, Ham and Swiss
Squeeze, chop, and finely grate.

I think the quiches are better if you lightly mix the filling ingredients (like toss bacon and Swiss) before putting into the pie shells. I have also found that they seem to cook best at about 365 degrees for 15 minutes or so. Check after 10 minutes. These don't have to be very brown if you are making them ahead (please do make them ahead). Freeze or store in fridge. Reheat them in batches as needed for your party.

Mini Puffs

These are really fussy and a pain to make but are well worth the trouble and will be a hit at your next party. This recipe makes 40-50 puffs to be filled with your favorite salads or the ones below.

Puffs

1 cup water
1 stick unsalted butter
1/4 tsp. salt
1 cup flour
4 eggs

Put water, butter, and salt into a heavy little saucepan and bring to a boil. Remove from heat and add flour, mixing with a wooden spoon, until smooth. Return to heat and cook, stirring constantly, until it becomes a smooth mass and the pan is coated with a fine film. This means the flour is cooked.

Remove from heat and transfer to mixer or processor bowl and let cool a little. Add eggs, one at a time, mixing until the batter is very smooth after each addition.

If egg is not completely mixed in at this point, you will have too thin a mixture. Just pay attention and be sure each egg is really mixed in well. Drop by heaping tablespoons onto a greased cookie sheet a few inches apart. It's a lot easier if you use two spoons and roll the mixture onto sheet.

Bake in a PREHEATED oven at 425 degrees for 10 minutes and reduce heat to 375 degrees and cook until nicely browned (about 20 minutes). Reduce heat to 325 and let bake 8 to 10 more minutes or until centers are dry. Don't open oven door until you reduce heat to 325 or they may fall.

I told you it was easy! Let cool and when it's almost time for the party you can fill with one or two of the fillings. Just cut tops and fill. I like to leave each top slightly attached and press back on lightly, after filling.

Fillings

Chicken Salad

Use your favorite recipe but cut chicken, celery, etc. finer than you would for a forked salad. We used chicken, celery, salt, white pepper, toasted sliced almonds (chopped a little), lemon juice, and mayonnaise.

Ham Salad

Trim ham of all fat, cut into cubes, process in batches, and empty into a bowl, adding well-drained sweet pickle relish and mayonnaise.

Crab Salad

Pick over fresh, frozen, or canned crab meat. Add diced celery, green onion, sweet red pepper, fresh parsley, mayonnaise, lemon juice, Old Bay, salt, pepper, and a couple of dashes of Tabasco.

Egg Salad

Make as usual, but add a little curry powder and pickle relish.

Puffs can be filled ahead of time and chilled, but I don't think they taste as good.

Hot Sausage Biscuits

3 cups Bisquick
1 pound sharp cheddar cheese, grated and at room temp.
1 pound bulk hot sausage

Mix well and roll into 1-1/2 inch balls and press down. Bake 20 minutes at 375 degrees. This is that old Southern Faithful. If you don't press them down, you can call them your famous sausage balls. This mixture can also be used to stuff and bake mushrooms.

Never get drunk and pass out
at your own party.
That's in bad taste.
Do it at your least likable
friend's house.

Cheese Straws

My grandchild, Emily, loved these the last time I made them. We hid them, just for us, from the over-Thanksgiving guests. Every hostess in the South seems to have a wonderful recipe for these. I found these in an old South Carolina cookbook, which was a gift from my sister, Peg. Thanks, Peg.

1 cup butter, softened
1 pound sharp cheddar cheese, grated and at room temp.
2-1/2 cups flour
1/2 tsp. cayenne pepper
1 tsp. salt
1 tsp. baking powder

Mix cheese and butter well, adding the mixed dry ingredients. Press through a cookie press (with a wide, flat tip) onto an ungreased cookie sheet, or you can form into balls and place on sheet, pressing with a fork, like cookies. Bake at 350 degrees for 10-15 minutes, but watch carefully to prevent overbaking. Store in an airtight container. Yields 14 to 16 dozen.

Parmesan Twists

I package frozen puff pastry sheets
Melted butter
Lawry's Seasoned Salt
Grated parmesan cheese

Let pastry sheets thaw. Place on a surface that has been sprinkled with some of the salt and parmesan cheese. Brush the surface of each sheet with the melted butter and sprinkle well with the salt and cheese. Using a pizza cutter or knife, cut each sheet in half the long way. Cut across into pieces about 3/4-inch wide. Twist each piece, holding one end between thumb and forefinger and twist three to four times. Lay each on a sprayed cookie sheet, making sure each end lies flat on the sheet. Bake 10 to 12 minutes in a 400 degree oven or until nicely browned and puffed. I think it is always best to do a few as a test batch on anything like these just to check on the size and your oven. Serve warm or at room temperature.

Walnut Cheese Cookies

These are so good and different to serve any time. Good conversation piece for a party.

8 ounces butter, softened
1 cup finely grated sharp white cheddar cheese (don't skimp on the cheese) at room temp.
1/4 tsp. salt
1/3 cup sugar
Dash of cayenne pepper
2-1/2 cups flour
1/2 cup chopped walnuts

Mix dry ingredients. Cream the cheese and butter together. Add dry ingredients to creamed mixture and combine well. Roll into walnut-sized balls and press with a fork. Bake at 350 degrees 10-12 minutes.

SQUARE PICKUPS

Artichoke Appetizers

1/2 cup chopped onion

2 or 3 dashes hot sauce

2 Tbs. butter

2 cups grated cheddar cheese

4 beaten eggs

1 can artichokes, drained and diced

1/4 cup dry bread crumbs

1/2 tsp. salt

1/8 tsp. each of pepper and oregano

Saute onion in the butter. Mix the rest, add the onion and spread in a greased 8x8 square pan. Bake at 350 degrees for 20-30 minutes. Cut into squares, the size you would like, and serve. Double for a 9x13 pan.

When my son was little
he had trouble saying his m's.
One day he said,
"Nonnie, you're a good cooker."

Laurie's
Spinach Appetizers

Laurie made these for Bunco and I fell in love.

10-ounce package of frozen chopped spinach, thawed and squeezed dry
1 pound grated sharp cheddar cheese
1 cup milk
1 cup flour
1 tsp. salt and 1 Tbs. baking powder
1 medium onion, chopped
1 stick butter, melted
2 beaten eggs

Mix all dry ingredients together and add to the mixed wet ones. Put into square 9x9 pan and bake at 350 degrees for 35 minutes. Cut into squares and serve warm. You can also bake in a medium-sized rectangular glass casserole dish.

Chili Cheese Squares

These are so good you will cry.

1 pound grated cheddar cheese
1-1/2 pounds grated Monterey Jack cheese
(about half with hot peppers)
2 4-ounce cans well-drained, chopped green chilies

Mix and put into a greased 9x13 pan or glass casserole.

6 eggs
6 Tbs. milk
3 Tbs. flour

Mix and pour over the cheese mixture in casserole and bake at 375 degrees for 45–50 minutes. Let cool and cut into small squares. This is even better if you make ahead, mark into squares, and reheat.

SPREAD-ON BREAD PICKUPS

Artichoke Bubbles

I'll bet we sold a million of these and I would also bet that Creative Cuisine still sells them.

16 slices of party rye or 2-inch bread rounds
1 14-ounce can of well-drained artichokes, cut in half
2 egg whites
4 Tbs. parmesan cheese, grated
2 Tbs. mayonnaise
2 Tbs. finely grated cheddar cheese
Dash of cayenne pepper

Toast bread on cookie sheet.

Beat egg whites until stiff and gently fold in mayo, cheeses, and cayenne. Lightly spread a little of mixture on each piece of toast and top with artichoke half, cut side down. Spread remaining topping on each, mounding to form bubble. Bake 10–15 minutes at 400 degrees until golden brown. For parties, we sent the toast rounds, the cut artichokes, and the topping separately with instructions on how to assemble and bake. We suggested this when we had our service people working a party.

Canapés

These are anything you would like to spread on those little cutout breads your cookie cutters limit you to making. Can use any crackers you have, but remember that they get soggy in minutes, so serve them quickly.

A good canape is to put a nice amount of shrimp butter on a white bread (like Pepperidge Farm) round, garnish with a tiny shrimp and a dill or parsley sprig.

Sherri's Ishkabibbles

My daughter, Sherri, and Linda, my late niece, named these while Sherri was sharing this unnamed recipe with her cousin. I walked in with wet hair and said that I looked like the old comic, Ish K. Bibble. The name stuck and was written down like it sounds. Several years later, when I went to a party in Columbus, Ohio, these were served. When I told the hostess what we had named them, she said, "No, you didn't!" and showed me her recipe, named Ishkabibbles. Her niece, who lived in Cincinnati, had sent her this recipe. Sherri also lived in the Cincinnati area and they both had graduated from the University of Cincinnati. The naming took place in South Carolina. The hostess never did get it, but I say it's a small world and Sherri is a generous person.

1 pound bulk hot sausage
1 pound ground beef
1 pound Velveeta cheese, cubed
1 small grated or minced onion
Garlic powder
Dried parsley and any herbs you would like...basil...thyme....
Hot sauce
Party rye (buy two loaves)

Brown meats and onion. Add the cubed cheese and other things and taste for seasonings. Spread generously on the party rye and bake at 400 degrees about 10 minutes or until bubbly hot. Can also freeze them before baking.

Caribbean Chicken Roulades with Tropical Salsa

Really good and different! Serve them cold or at room temperature.

Butter 2-inch bread rounds. Sprinkle with sugar and cinnamon, put on cookie sheet, and toast. Allow 2 per person with other party foods.

8 chicken breast halves, pounded and trimmed of fat

Spreading Mixture
1/2 cup sugar
1 Tbs. curry powder
1 tsp. each of cinnamon, turmeric, allspice, salt, and ground ginger
1/2 tsp. cayenne pepper
4 Tbs. Hoisin sauce
1 Tbs. vegetable oil

Mix well and spread on chicken halves. Roll up the chicken from tip to top making a roll that, when cooked and sliced, will fit on those toast rounds. Use toothpicks to secure and cook until they test done. Chill until you are ready to assemble these little treasures.

Tropical Salsa

1 large tomato, seeded and diced
1 papaya, peeled, seeded, and diced
1 avocado, peeled, seeded, and diced
1/4 of a fresh pineapple, diced
3 green onions, finely diced
1 or 2 jalapeno peppers, seeded and finely diced
1/4 cup olive oil
2 Tbs. each of honey and lemon or lime juice
Chopped fresh cilantro or parsley
Salt and pepper to taste

Mix this up, taste, and adjust seasonings. You may like it to be hotter, so add cayenne pepper or more jalapeno peppers.

Slice chicken into 1/4-inch rounds and put on those toast rounds. Put a spoonful of salsa on top and garnish, if you like, with parsley or cilantro.

This makes a lot of salsa, but it's good on everything. As Daddy used to say, "This would even be good on a sore toe!"

My funny Daddy always had sage advice.
Never stand, if you can sit.
Never sit, if you can lie down.
Never buy, if you can borrow.
Never borrow, if you can steal.
Never tell the truth, if you can tell a lie.
Such words of wisdom....

Mary's Crab Boboli

Mary is the lady who started this whole catering business in which I became so deeply involved. She never did tell me, after my first job interview, if I was hired or not. She just made me keep working until Harold, her husband, forced her to sell the business to three of us. She ran away to Florida, where she is still missing the catering thing. So many of these recipes are straight from her collection. Thanks, I think, Mary.

1 small can good crab, drained
1/2 cup mayonnaise
1 cup grated Swiss cheese
1/8 tsp. curry powder
Chopped green onion
3 small Boboli shells

Mix all and spread on the shells. Bake at 425 degrees until hot and bubbly. Cut into wedges.

Remember to garnish everything nicely!

Pesto Pizzas

1 jar of your favorite pesto sauce
Olive oil
Grated parmesan cheese
Grated mozzarella cheese
Small Boboli shells

You will have to judge how many shells to buy based on the amount of pesto you buy. Put pesto in a bowl and add olive oil and parmesan cheese to make a nice pizza-type sauce. Spread on the shells and sprinkle on a generous amount of mozzarella. Bake at 425 degrees until hot and bubbly.

Cut in wedges and serve them up.

If your children or grandchildren are at the age when they say and do such adorable things, write them down. Otherwise, when they get to be teenagers, you won't be able to remember one cute thing they ever said or did.

STAB 'UMS

Round
Stab 'Ums

Spinach Balls

Don't know who created these, but they are great to
keep on hand in the freezer.

2 10-ounce packages of chopped frozen spinach,
thawed and squeezed dry
2 cups packaged stuffing mix
1 cup parmesan cheese
6 eggs, beaten well
1-1/2 sticks butter, melted
Salt and pepper.
Remember that the parmesan is salty.

Mix all, roll into balls, and bake on a greased cookie sheet at 350 degrees for 10-15 minutes. Can freeze and then bake frozen, but allow more time to bake.

Basic Meatballs

1 pound good ground beef
1 egg
1/2 cup dry bread crumbs
2 Tbs. finely diced or grated onion
1 tsp. salt
1/4 tsp. black pepper

Mix well, but keep it light and form into the size ball you like. I like to make them walnut size and get about 30 from a pound of mixture. Put on a cookie sheet that has been lined with foil and pan sprayed. Bake at 375 degrees for 10 minutes and serve in favorite sauce.

George's German Meatballs with Caper Sauce

I'm trying to forget George, my young man friend right after my divorce, but his German mamma was a great cook.

Meatballs

1 medium dinner roll
3/4 cup water
1 pound lean ground beef
1 strip bacon, finely diced
4 anchovy fillets, diced
1 small onion, chopped small
1 egg
1/2 tsp. salt and 1/4 tsp. white pepper

Broth

6 cups water
1 tsp. salt
1 Tbs. lemon juice
1 small bay leaf
1 small onion, peeled
6 peppercorns

Sauce

1-1/2 Tbs. butter
1-1/2 Tbs. flour
1 Tbs. capers
Juice of 1/2 lemon
1/2 tsp. Dijon mustard
1 egg yolk
1/4 tsp. each of salt and white pepper

Make the broth first and simmer, covered, while you form the meatballs. Soak the roll in the water for 10 minutes and squeeze dry. Add to ground beef and other ingredients for balls and mix well, but keep as light as possible. Form into 1-1/4-inch balls and simmer gently in broth for about 10 minutes. Remove with a slotted spoon and reserve broth.

Make sauce by heating butter, stir in flour and cook for 2-3 minutes. Stir constantly and add 2 cups of the reserved broth. Add the capers, lemon juice, and mustard. Let simmer for 5 minutes. Remove a little of the sauce to add to the beaten egg yolk and return mixture to sauce. Season with salt and pepper. Place meatballs in sauce and serve in a chafer for a party. Also good for dinner over noodles.

Never be rude to an invited guest.
Save that for the uninvited ones.

Cheater's Meatballs

Buy the number of frozen meatballs that you need for your party and put them in a bowl.

Add sauce made of 1/4 cup of orange marmalade to each cup of your favorite barbeque sauce and pour over meatballs. You don't want them swimming in sauce, but coat them well.

Stick the whole thing in the fridge to thaw. While they are thawing they are soaking up flavor from the sauce. You can do this a couple of days before your party and then just heat them up and put in a chafer. It is also pretty and good to drain pineapple chunks really well and put them in a circle around the sides of the chaffing dish on top of the meatballs. Serve with toothpicks to stab 'um.

Chicken Almond Puffs

My brother-in-law, Paul, made these for his daughter's wedding reception. I catered this party with his and my sister's help. Paul was to make these, cook them, put on baking sheets, freeze them, and then store in plastic bags. He started out fine with making and freezing, but when he got up to about 200, they got bigger and bigger until some looked like tennis balls when I saw them on the wedding day. They tasted wonderful!

2 cups finely chopped cooked chicken, use processor
1 cup mashed potatoes
1 egg, separated
1/2 tsp. each or salt and pepper
1 tsp. curry powder
1 to 2 Tbs. heavy cream
1/2 cup fine dry bread crumbs
1/2 cup finely ground almonds
oil for frying

Mix chicken, potatoes, egg yolk, salt, pepper, curry powder, and enough cream to moisten to roll into 1-inch balls. Dip into slightly beaten egg white and roll in the almond-bread-crumb mixture. Chill 30 minutes or more (you could freeze at this point) and fry in deep oil at 375 degrees until balls are crisp and golden. Serve or freeze like Paul did. Are good as is or you can serve with a mixture of mayonnaise and chopped Major Grey's chutney to dip.

STAB 'UMS IN BACON

I have found that it works best to do bacon wraps on a rack. If you have a convection oven, all the better. I line a large jelly roll pan with foil and place two cake cooling racks on foil. Spray really well with Pam and place bacon wraps on rack. These seem to cook well at 425 degrees. You may need to turn them, but with the rack, your chances are better that they won't need it. If you can't rig up a rack, spray your pan and gently crumple foil to hold the wraps up and let grease drain.

You will have to make the decision whether to use 1/2 piece or 1/3 piece of bacon, according to the size of that thing you are going to wrap. You want the bacon to overlap so you can stab it good. If reheating, don't cook until well done. Always preheat oven.

Water Chestnuts in Bacon

Whole canned water chestnuts, well drained
Soy sauce
Brown sugar
Ground ginger

Put chestnuts in a container with a well-fitting lid. Use enough of the mentioned ingredients to at least half cover. Put in fridge to marinate overnight or for a couple of days. Remember to shake it up a few times. Wrap 'um, stab 'um, cook 'um, and eat 'um.

Dates in Bacon

My son, Bud, thinks if you have water chestnuts in bacon, you have to have dates in bacon.

Whole pitted dates (can soak in brandy for an hour or so)
Bacon
Almonds or nuts if you would like to stuff them in the dates

These burn very easily so you will want to stay close and watch them carefully. Bake as directed above, but you may want to turn the oven down if yours tends to brown things quickly.

Olives in Bacon

Biggest stuffed green olives you can find
1/3 or 1/2 piece of bacon each
Toothpicks

Wrap, stab, and cook. They are salty but really good.

World's Best Chicken Livers in Bacon

1 pound chicken livers, rinsed, trimmed, cut in half
1/2 cup yellow mustard
1/4 cup finely minced stuffed green olives
Plain bread crumbs with a little salt and pepper added
1/2 piece of bacon for each liver section

Mix mustard and olives in a flat bowl. Put bread crumbs in another flat bowl. Drop livers into mustard mixture and stir around to coat. Drop coated livers into the crumbs to coat. If you are lucky and use tongs, you won't have to touch these until they are well coated with crumbs. Wrap in bacon, secure with a pick, and bake on rack in 425 degrees oven until bacon is crispy.

Spicy Oysters in Bacon

Drain the oysters well and sprinkle with Old Bay, a little lemon juice, and Tabasco to taste.

Stick the whole thing back in fridge for a couple of hours.

Wrap with bacon. (You may have to taste at this point. If they are really good, put the bacon away and turn off the oven.)

Bake at 425 degrees and serve them up.

I would not do these ahead of time to reheat.

Shauna's Bacon and Cheese Rollups

Shauna was one of my slightly redneck, but beautiful, catering business partners. I had three partners and they all fit that description, but Shauna was the one who loved these from her childhood.

Cheap white loaf bread, trimmed and rolled flat with a rolling pin
Jar of that sharp processed cheese spread
Bacon halves and those toothpicks

Spread the cheese on the bread, roll up, cut into thirds, wrap, and bake them. If you cover the cut ends of the bread with the bacon, the cheese stays in better. Shauna never did that, but melted, baked cheese is great when you scoop it up with some of the bacon grease.

Just kidding, Shauna....you know I love you!

Barbequed Shrimp in Bacon

Big raw shrimp
Prepared horseradish
Open Pit (or your favorite) barbeque sauce
Bacon halves

Butterfly or cut raw shrimp down the back. Cut deeper than you would when cleaning them. Put in as much horseradish as you think you can stand and brush well with barbeque sauce. Wrap them in bacon, secure with pick, and bake at 425 degrees until you think shrimp are done. These are good!

SKEWERED STAB 'UMS

These, of course, are the ones you stab with a bigger stick and usually put more stuff on the stick. Most are marinated and basted with some of the leftover marinade.

I don't know why, but food does seem to taste better if you go to all that trouble to put it on that stick.

Almost anything can be put on those skewers. Shrimp, scallops, beef, lamb, even precooked meatballs. onions, pearl onions, peppers, squashes, cherry tomatoes, mushrooms, and eggplant are a few of the skewerable items you can use, and all skewered things don't even have to be cooked....

Karen's Asian Chicken Kabobs

My daughter, Karen, created these a few years ago and they have become one of our favorites. Good served as an entree too.

1/3 cup Hoisin sauce
1 2-inch long piece gingerroot, peeled and grated
2 Tbs. rice vinegar
2 Tbs. soy sauce
2 Tbs. dry sherry
1 Tbs. peanut oil
1 clove of crushed garlic
1/2 tsp. of grated lemon rind
1-1/2 pounds of boned chicken breasts, trimmed well and cut in 1-inch pieces.
1 chopped green onion for garnish

Skewers can be any length, but remember to soak in water for a while to prevent burning.

Mix the sauce things well and add the chicken pieces to marinate for 10 minutes or so. Don't marinate longer than an hour or meat will get a mealy texture. Put chicken pieces on skewers but save marinade to baste with. Put skewers on a foil-lined pan and broil for 2 minutes. Brush with marinade and turn skewers over and brush other side. Broil 2 more minutes and test for doneness. Sprinkle with green onions and serve on a pretty tray that has been lined with shredded greens.

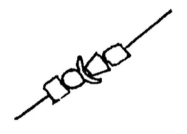

Scotch Lemon Chicken Skewers

8 boneless chicken breast halves,
cut into 1-1/2 inch pieces
1/3 cup Scotch
1/3 cup honey
1/3 cup soy sauce
1/2 cup vegetable oil
Salt and pepper
2 lemons, scored and sliced
24 large mushrooms
12 large green onions, cut up to fit skewers
1 large each, red and green pepper,
cut into 1-1/2 inch squares

Marinate all of this overnight in a plastic bag or shakable plastic container. Put on skewers that have been soaked in water. Cook on grill or in oven, basting with the marinade, until chicken is done. The lemons stay on skewers better if you fold them over. This makes about 16 skewers or more, according to the size you want them.

Italian Sausage and Pepper Skewers

Italian sausage in casing, links or rope style
Red, yellow, and green bell peppers
Mild onions
Red wine and olive oil

Precook the sausage in the oven or a skillet with a little water, just until it is done enough to cut into sections to go on skewers. Cut peppers and onions into pieces to fit on skewers. I think that one inch is too small so I usually go with about one and a half inch pieces. Marinate for an hour or so with some red wine and olive oil. Put on skewers and grill or cook in oven, basting with oil and wine.

Myrt's Shrimp

Myrt was my best friend and she never knew why I didn't keep in touch when I moved. I haven't forgotten her or these good shrimp.

1 pound raw shrimp, cleaned and shelled
1 clove garlic, crushed
1/2 cup olive oil
1 tsp. salt and lots of freshly cracked black pepper
3 Tbs. chili sauce
1 Tbs. Worcestershire sauce
3 Tbs. vinegar
1/4 cup fresh, chopped parsley
Tabasco to taste

Mix sauce ingredients and pour over shrimp that you have rinsed and put into a glass bowl. Marinate overnight or at least four hours. Place on soaked skewers and broil or cook on the grill. These are good and I am going to try to get in touch with Myrt!

COLD SKEWERED STAB 'UMS

Consider ye ole fruit skewers or the old ham and cheese cubes with an olive.

Another good cold one is cooked, tri-colored tortellini, skewered and brushed with Italian dressing. Serve with a pesto dip or mayonnaise thinned with Italian dressing.

How about marinated artichokes that you drain very well, Italian cheese cubes, pepperoni pieces, pickled peppers, basil leaves, cherry or grape tomatoes? Antipasto on a stick!

Or banana sections dipped in fruit flavored yogurt or sweetened sour cream and rolled in shredded coconut. Add a few strawberries and you have a beautiful skewer.

Melon balls make a nice skewer. Mary used to always insist on balls until we realized how much fruit we were wasting. We all felt compelled to eat up those holey melon halves. We had to spend more time eating than we did working.

One time, when I answered the phone at Creative Cuisine, an office girl asked if we made those Chicken Kaboobs. We always called skewered things Kaboobs after that. Sometimes it's hard to have fun and work too.

MISCELLANEOUS FAVORITES

The next two recipes came from
The Silver Palate cookbooks but have
been changed around, of course. Get
those first two books, The Silver Palate
and The Silver Palate Good Times.
They are great!

Spinach and Walnut Stuffed Mushrooms

24 medium-sized mushrooms
2 Tbs. melted butter
2 Tbs. olive oil
2 Tbs. butter
1 cup finely chopped onion
1/3 cup chopped walnuts
1 or 2 cloves minced garlic
1 10-ounce box of frozen chopped spinach, thawed and squeezed dry
2 ounces crumbled feta cheese
2 ounces grated Gruyere or strong Swiss cheese
2 Tbs. minced fresh dill (use less if you use dried)
Salt and pepper to taste

Remove stems from mushrooms and save if you'd like. (Can throw them away the next time you find them in the fridge hidden behind the moldy beans from a couple of weeks ago.)

Brush the mushrooms with a damp cloth, brush with melted butter, and set aside.

Preheat oven to 400 degrees. Heat the olive oil and butter in a small skillet. Add the onions and cook slowly until limp and add the garlic and walnuts and cook another few minutes. Remove from heat and add the squeezed spinach, cheeses, dill, and salt and pepper to taste.

Divide the mixture evenly into the mushroom caps and bake in upper part of oven for 8-10 minutes or until nicely browned. These can be made ahead of time, refrigerated, and cooked right before you serve them.

Cajun Chicken Bites

1-1/2 cups plain flour
1 cup finely chopped pecans
1 tsp. dried oregano
2 tsp. ground cumin
1 tsp. dried thyme
1/2 tsp. cayenne pepper
Salt to taste
1 stick butter
10 boneless, skinless chicken breasts, cut into 1-inch pieces

Mix the dry ingredients in a shallow bowl. Melt the butter, dip the chicken in it, and then roll in the flour mixture. Place on a Pam-sprayed cookie sheet and spray chicken pieces with Pam. Bake at 400 degrees for 5 minutes and check to see if they need to be turned and sprayed again. Cook for another 5 minutes and check for doneness. Can be reheated, but don't let them get too brown when you first cook them.

Fresh flowers make a wonderful garnish, but always make sure they are edible.

Maria's Creamy Pickled Herring

Maria brought this for Thanksgiving and I fell in love again. Maria is Don's mother. Don is Sherri's love and Sherri is my daughter. Sherri and Don live in Atlanta with their three cats. Maria and Andy, Don's father and Maria's husband, live in New Jersey, and they all come here every Thanksgiving and then Don's sister and her...hell...the story is too long. Just come for Thanksgiving and I won't have to finish the story. We have a great time.

1 jar pickled herring (equal to about 2 cups), drained
1 cup sour cream
2 or 3 Tbs. mayonnaise
1 cup Granny Smith apple, peeled and chopped
1 small sweet onion, thinly sliced
Salt and pepper if you like

Mix all and store in a glass or plastic container until ready to serve. Put into a pretty bowl and serve garnished nicely. It would be pretty to garnish this with a few apple slices that have been dipped in lemon juice or Fruit Fresh.

Serve with crackers or party rye.

Cecil and Walt's Ceviche

My brother, Walt, and his wife, Cecil, brought this to the beach at the same time as Cecil's Peking Pecans and it was greatly enjoyed. We spent nine days taking turns with cooking meals along with serving all the many other goodies that we tried to outdo each other with. Sister Peg even cooked our Christmas dinner in February. We had a real eat-a-thon and I loved it.

1-1/2 pounds fillet of red snapper or other firm, white fish, diced
3/4 cup lemon juice
1/2 to 3/4 cup dry white wine

Put all into a nonreactive bowl and marinate ovenight in refrigerator. Make sauce, add to fish and chill well before serving.

Sauce
4 tomatoes, peeled and diced
1 onion, finely diced
30 chopped stuffed green olives
1 cup catsup

1/4 cup chopped fresh parsley
3 jalapeno peppers, diced
1 green pepper, diced
Salt and pepper to taste

Serve in a pretty bowl with crackers or provide little shells and fish forks for individual cocktail servings.

Our Clams Casino

When we have steamed clams, I save the shells for this. I couldn't find a recipe so Karen and I created these. We liked them so much that I wrote everything down. Remember to do that when you make something you like.

1/2 cup finely minced onion
1/2 cup finely minced celery
1/2 cup finely minced green pepper
4 Tbs. butter
1/2 cup fresh bread crumbs (stick a couple of slices of bread in freezer and then grate like you would cheese)
2 or 3 Tbs. grated parmesan
1/2 tsp. Worcestershire sauce
1 tsp. Old Bay
Juice of 1/2 lemon
Tabasco to taste
2 or 3 6-ounce cans minced clams, drain but save juice
Salt and pepper to taste

Melt butter in a medium skillet and saute the vegetables until limp but not brown. Add all the other stuff, taste, and adjust seasonings. If it seems dry you can add some of that saved clam juice until you think it is right for stuffing in those above-mentioned saved and pan-sprayed shells. Bake at 400 degrees for 10 minutes or until they are hot, browned, and bubbly.

My Oysters Rockefeller

24-36 large raw oysters, shucked if you remember to save some shells
10-ounce package frozen chopped spinach, thawed and squeezed dry
1 stalk chopped celery
6 chopped green onions
1/2 cup chopped fresh parsley
1 Tbs. Worcestershire sauce
1 Tbs. anchovy paste
1/2 tsp. anise seed
1/4 cup fresh bread crumbs
1/8 cup grated parmesan cheese
1 stick of melted butter
Tabasco, salt and pepper to taste
Rock salt or crumpled foil

Process the green things and place in a bowl. Add the rest of the items but not the oysters, rock salt, or the foil. Mix lightly to combine everything.

Put oysters in a pan and heat just until they release some liquid and the edges just start to curl. Drain on paper towels and place one oyster in each shell half that has been put on the rock salt or the crumpled foil to secure them.

Top each with the spinach mixture and run under the broiler until bubbly brown.

Good...good...good!

I have also made this into a casserole.

My Pickled Shrimp

I combined several recipes and came up with this recipe that I really like and have made for years. Feel free to add your own touches but do allow two days for the flavors to marry.

2 pounds cooked and cleaned cocktail-sized shrimp
4 Tbs. olive oil
2 Tbs. tarragon vinegar
1 tsp. salt
Cayenne pepper to taste
1 tsp. dry mustard
1 tsp. sugar
Juice of 1/2 lemon or more
2 Tbs. pickling spices
2 small bay leaves
1 or 2 thinly sliced white onions
1 large can of well-drained, pitted black olives

Mix the marinade ingredients and add the shrimp, onions, and olives. Put into glass or plastic, shakable lidded container. Remember to move those shrimp around while they are marinating, tasting and adding to the seasoning as you go.

It's a good idea to allow a few extra shrimp since you will be testing them for a couple of days. I lift them out of the marinade and serve them in a pretty bowl. I like to put a serving spoon on the side along with little plates and toothpicks or cocktail forks.

Potted Cheese and Bacon

3 8-ounce packages of sharp processed cheese
1 pound bacon, fried crisp, drained well and crumbled
1 bunch green onions, chopped (I always include tops or why buy them?)

Cut cheese into 1/4-inch cubes and mix with bacon and onions. Pack into an earthenware-type crock or casserole. Bake at 400 degrees for 20 minutes.

Salmon Crab Cakes with Papaya Caper Sauce

8 ounces salmon, freshly cooked or leftover cooked
8 ounces lump crab, picked over
3 green onions, mince both parts
2 Tbs. chopped fresh parsley
1/4 cup cracker meal
1/4 cup mayonnaise
1 tsp. Dijon mustard
1 Tbs. fresh lemon juice
1 egg, beaten
Cracker meal, to dredge cakes
Vegetable oil, for frying

Flake salmon and add the other ingredients, mix well but keep mixture light. Form into small cakes, roll in cracker meal, and fry in the oil. Drain on paper towels and serve with the following sauce:

Papaya Caper Sauce

1/2 cup plain yogurt
1/2 cup mayonnaise
1 Tbs. drained chopped capers
1 Tbs. chopped cilantro or dill
1/2 cup chopped papaya

These can be made ahead and reheated, before adding sauce, at 350 degrees, just until heated through. One recipe should make at least 30 cakes.

* * *

Well, enough is enough. I have more recipes, but I think you will be able to do a few parties with these.

Remember to choose a nice variety of things for your menu. Serve some hot and some cold, some meat and some seafood, some fruit and some vegetables. Fruit and cheese trays are almost as good as those antipasto trays.

Do as much of the food ahead of time as possible so you can enjoy those friends and family that you cared about enough to ask to your party.

Don't invite anyone that you don't like. They will hopefully stop asking you after a while.

It's always a good idea to have a few little sweet things around for your guests. Do make the pieces small and pretty. Little compotes of great candy that you purchase are a good start.

Just have fun!

AFTERWORD

It's been over ten years since our mother wrote *The Old Caterer's Favorite Hors d'oeuvres,* and she has continued to entertain and provide our family and friends with her fabulous, expertly presented food. Mother always intended to follow this book with a series of course-themed books. The next was to be *Soups and Salads,* for which she has a kitchen drawer chock full of wonderful recipes. However, as years passed, she decided she had put all her eggs in her first book, and settled in with this being her claim to fame.

In celebration of Dot's eightieth birthday this fall, we decided to release a brand new edition, hence this very printing. How exciting to turn eighty and see your life's work in print. Those of you who already own this book know how simple and wonderful the recipes are. It's hard to have a party without using at least one.

Thanksgiving continues to be our biggest hors d'oeuvre blowout...and although we've added a few new ones to the table — and vary what we do from year to year — we've yet to go a year without *Our Clam Dip* (page 10), *Dill Sauce for Salmon* (page 27), and mother's antipasto tray (page 63). We lost Maria to colon cancer in 2006 (*Maria's Creamy Pickled Herring,* page 131), but the memory of her pickled herring and how much she loved the Thanksgiving hors d'oeuvres lives on.

One final Dot story: please refer to *Karen's Asian Chicken Kabobs* (page

118). When my sister, Karen, read mother's draft back in early 2000 and saw that mother had given her credit for "creating" the recipe, she quickly reminded her that she had *not*—that it was taken word for word from one of the cookbooks Karen owned. Mother shrugged it off and responded, "Well, I wanted to include you in the book, and that's all I could come up with! It doesn't matter; this will never be published." But now that it is, Karen would like to give credit where credit is due, but of course, has no idea now where the original recipe came from. So, sorry…. Great recipe, Karen. Guess it's officially yours now!

—Sherri

The Dot Winters, a.k.a. The Old Caterer

INDEX

A

Antipasto:

Artichoke(s):

B

Bacon:

F

Fillings:
for puffs, 71
for quiche, 69

Fruit kabobs, 123

G

Grapes, Roquefort, 64

H

Herring, Maria's creamy pickled, 131

Hummus bi Tahini, 7

I

Ishkabibbles, Sherri's, 88

J

K

L

Lemon chicken skewers, Scott, 120

M

N

O

Olives in bacon, 112

Oysters:
  Rockefeller, 137
  spicy in bacon, 114

P

Papaya caper sauce, 142

Parmesan twists, 76

Pâté:
  Chicken liver, 59
  Mushroom, 53

Pecans, Peking, 65

Peppers and sausage skewers, 121

Pizzas:
  Crab Boboli, 93
  Pesto, 95
Puffs:
  chicken almond, 106
  mini, 70

Q

Queso, chili con, 19

V

Vegetables:
>on antipasto tray, 63
>in caponata, 55
>in cucumber dip, 5
>with dill dip, 3
>with spinach dip, 9

W

Walnut:
>in cheese cookies, 77
>and spinach stuffed mushrooms, 127

Water chestnuts in bacon, 110

X

Y

Yogurt in caper sauce, 143

Z

Zucchini in caponata, 55

CPSIA information can be obtained at www.ICGtesting.com
Printed in the USA
267297BV00004B/4/P